Contents

Sounds in this book

aw (outlaw) ea (real, dead) ear (years)
eer (deer) g (legend) ture (adventures)
o (money) ore (wore)

Tales of long ago

Do you know the story of Robin Hood? He stole money from the rich and gave it to the poor.

There are lots of books, TV shows and films about Robin Hood.

The stories are set about 800 years ago. Could these tales be true, or is Robin Hood just a **legend**?

THE LIFE AND ADVENTURES OF ROBIN HOOD

There have been stories about Robin Hood for a long time!

Robin Hood

Different stories tell us different things about Robin. Some stories say he started off as a rich man.

An actor playing a rich man at the time of Robin Hood

But then Prince John stole his land, so Robin went to Sherwood Forest, near the city of Nottingham.

It's true!

There is a Sherwood Forest. You can visit it.

Welcome to
SHERWOOD FOREST COUNTRY PARK

Nottinghamshire County Council
Leisure Services

Robin the outlaw

Sherwood Forest was a royal forest, and all the deer in the forest were the king's. But Robin broke the law! He hunted and ate the deer.

It's true!

In the past, if you broke the law you were called an outlaw.

Robin made people stop as they went into the forest. If they were rich, he stole their money and gave it to poor people.

Meet Robin Hood

The stories tell us that Robin Hood always wore green clothes. He always had a hunting horn and a bow and arrow.

Robin was brave and very crafty. He got into a lot of fights, but he did not always win!

Robin Hood was very good at shooting arrows.

9

Look out, Robin Hood!

Robin sometimes went into Nottingham in secret, to enter **archery** contests. He always got first prize.

Now and then, Robin was spotted and thrown into prison in Nottingham Castle. Luckily, he had lots of people to help him get out!

Help arrives for Robin!

The Merry Men

Robin's followers were called the Merry Men. The stories tell us about their adventures.

Robin and the Merry Men enjoy a feast.

When Robin needed help he blew his horn three times. Then the Merry Men came to rescue him!

Robin Hood could have used a hunting horn like this.

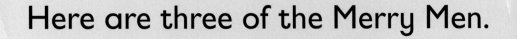

Here are three of the Merry Men.

Little John was very tall! He was Robin's right-hand man.

Friar Tuck was jolly and very fond of eating.

Maid Marian was Robin's true love.

Maid Marian was not a Merry **Man**!

Robin's enemy

Robin Hood had an enemy. His name was the Sheriff of Nottingham. The Sheriff wanted to catch Robin – dead or alive!

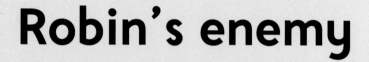

Robin Hood and the Sheriff of Nottingham

Luckily, Robin always beat the wicked Sheriff. Sometimes, he even got the Sheriff's gold!

It's true!

The Sheriff was the most important person in Nottingham.

The end of the story

The stories say that in the end the king forgave Robin and gave him back his land.

Robin's last arrow

At the end of his life, when Robin Hood was very old, he shot an arrow out of his window. His grave was dug where the arrow fell.

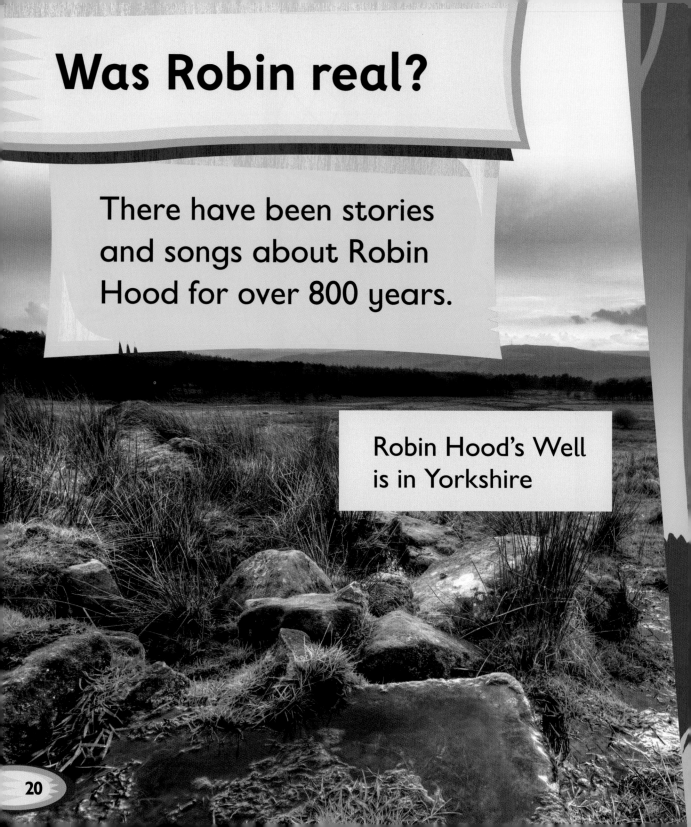

Was Robin real?

There have been stories and songs about Robin Hood for over 800 years.

Robin Hood's Well is in Yorkshire

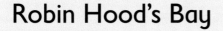

Robin Hood's Bay

I hope Robin Hood was real!

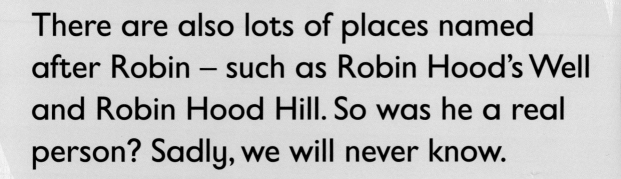

There are also lots of places named after Robin – such as Robin Hood's Well and Robin Hood Hill. So was he a real person? Sadly, we will never know.

Robin Hood today

Robin Hood and his adventures are still popular today. You can read them or watch them in films and on television.

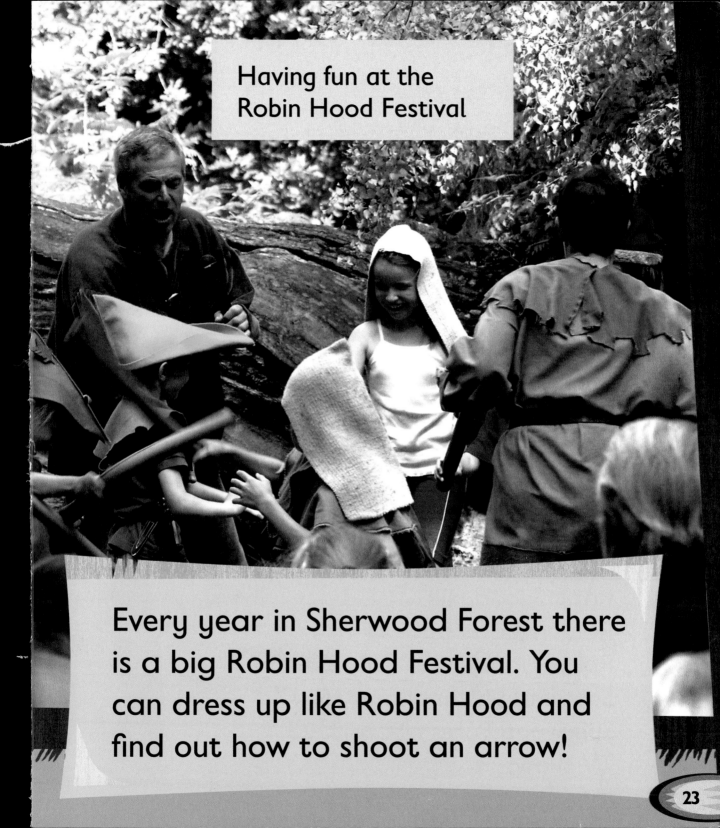

Having fun at the
Robin Hood Festival

Every year in Sherwood Forest there
is a big Robin Hood Festival. You
can dress up like Robin Hood and
find out how to shoot an arrow!

Glossary

Archery: a sport where you use a bow and arrow

Friar: a man of the church

Legend: a story that is probably not true

Index